A PARTIER'S
GUIDE TO
51 DRINKING
GAMES

BY BRIAN L. PELLHAM

Edited by Amy Neises
Illustrations by Nate Manny

Special thanks to Allison Kent, Cory Koski, Emily Ross
Carl Brogli, Erich Schneider, Tony Pellham, Joan Yarkosky,
Mark Gustafson, and Heather Wood for their contributions.

Inquiries should be addressed to:
Kheper Publishing
P.O. Box 906
Bellevue, WA 98009-0906

Printed and bound in China

DEDICATED TO EMILY ROSS

TABLE OF CONTENTS

INTRODUCTION

It's finally the weekend. After spending five days (and let's not talk about how many hours) in either a job you hate or in boring classes, you're more than ready to embrace the weekend's festivities. As you begin discussing your plans with your friends, you consider taking a walk in the park, watching a movie, or even having an intimate discussion about Nietzsche's philosophies. Eventually you all realize that what you really want to do is hang out with your friends and play a few drinking games. But then you're faced with trying to decide what game to play. Relying on your memories of past games you've played leaves you with a limited set of games to choose from, many to which you can't remember all of the rules. Fortunately, "A Partier's Guide to 51 Drinking Games" offers you the rules of play for several old favorites (Quarters, Asshole, etc.) and many new games (Preposterous Proposal, Assembly Line, etc.). So sit back, mix up your favorite drink, and put away your breakables--the party is about to begin!

NOT RECOMMENDED TO BE PLAYED WITH ALCOHOL.

GENERAL RULES

There are a few general rules that apply to all games.

 **BEVERAGE CONSUMPTION RATING**

Next to the title of each game is a rating, which indicates the average number of drinks that players can expect to consume during a half hour of play. Each mug in the rating represents one 12 ounce drink. The ratings for each game range from one to five mugs, which corresponds to the average number of 12 ounce beverages that a player could expect to be consuming for each half hour of play. If a five mug rating is followed by a '+' then each player should expect to consume more than five drinks per half hour. It is important for all players to realize that the rating is an **average**, this figure may vary significantly depending on the number of players and on the game.

It is recommended that these games be played with nonalcoholic beverages. If players do decide to play these games with alcohol, they should carefully determine how many drinks they can safely consume before starting a game. **IMPORTANT...** A player should ignore a drink assignment and quit a game if taking the drink causes the player to exceed his or her set limit. Games with three or more mugs should not be played with alcoholic beverages. If players insist on playing these games with alcohol then the drink penalties should be reduced.

WHO GOES FIRST

Unless the game mentions a specific method, it is up to the players to determine who initiates the first round of play. Possible methods are:

- Highest roll*: all players roll dice, the highest roll goes first.
- Highest card*: all players draw a card, the highest card goes first.
- Chug a drink: all players chug a drink, the fastest chugger goes first.
- Loudest armpit noise

* If two or more players tie (with the highest card/roll), then those players should draw or roll again.

Additional Methods (Two Player Games Only)

- Rock, Scissors, Paper (see rules on page 90)
- Coin flip (the coin may be substituted with other objects, such as a condom, bottlecap, or the smallest player)

MISTAKES (PARTY FOULS)

The penalty for an error should be one drink. Mistakes should be defined by the group members before playing, or when they arise. Examples of actions that should be defined as mistakes are:

- Sloppy dice: rolling the dice off the table
- Misdeal: dealing the cards out of order or skipping players

- Sloppy quarter: bouncing the quarter off the table

- Playing out of turn

- Falling out of your chair

- Other mistakes: as mentioned in the rules section of the particular

  game

QUARTERS, ETC.

QUARTERS

Number of Players 2 +

Setup

All that is needed for this game is a quarter and a shot glass. Players should be seated around a hard-surfaced table. The shot glass should be placed in the center of the table. If all players cannot easily reach the glass here, then it should be placed in front of the player who is selected to go first.

Play

Players have one chance to bounce the quarter off the table and into the shot glass. If the player misses, then she passes the shot glass and quarter to the next person. If she bounces the quarter into the glass, she can then assign a drink to another player of her choice and she can take another turn. If she is successful three times in a row she gets to make a rule (see Appendix A for sample rules). The rule can be anything that governs how the game is played, as long as it applies to all players. The player continues taking turns until she misses. She is able to make a second rule after the sixth success, a third rule after the ninth, and so on.

Tips on Bouncing the Quarter

Hold the quarter between your thumb and pointer finger. It should be horizontal and about six inches above the table. Use a quick, jerking motion when you throw it down to the table. The height of the bounce will vary depending on the surface of the table (the quarter should not bounce more than a couple of inches above the shot glass).

12

Variations

One option is for a player to cancel any existing rule that she may not care for, instead of making a new rule after three successes. Also, a play may include a rim shot dare. If a player misses his shot but catches the rim of the shot glass he can take another turn. However, if he misses again on his second attempt then he must drink and his turn ends.

CHANDELIERS

Number of Players 2+

Setup

Place a large glass in the center of the table. Then place shot glasses in a circle around the center glass. The rims of the shot glasses should touch each other and the center glass. All glasses should be empty.

Play

Players take turns trying to bounce quarters into any one of the glasses. When a player makes one into a shot glass, he can assign a drink to another player. If the quarter lands into the center glass, then he can pour some of his drink into it. If he makes a quarter into any glass then he gets to take another turn. If a player is successful at landing his quarter into a shot glass three times in a row, then he can tell someone to drink the center drink (or a replacement beverage if the drinker does not want a drink that contains quarter grime). Landing the quarter into the center cup does not count as one of these three shots. The player's turn ends when he misses. At this point, the quarter must be passed to the next player. Only one player should be bouncing a quarter at a time.

For tips on bouncing the quarter and variations see the rules for Quarters.

DAREDEVIL

Number of Players 2+

Setup

Five shot glasses need to be lined up in a row with their rims touching each other.

Play

Players take turns trying to bounce quarters into the shot glasses. When a player takes a turn she needs to be sitting so that the shot glasses are in a straight line in front of her. If the player makes the quarter into the first glass, then she can assign one drink, two drinks if it lands into the second glass, etc. If the player makes it into the fifth glass then she may assign five drinks or make up a rule (see Appendix A for sample rules). The assigned drinks can be split between players. The rule can be anything that governs how the game is played as long as it applies to all players and each player is allowed only one attempt per turn.

SPEED QUARTERS

Number of Players 4+

Setup

Two quarters and two shot glasses are needed. Two players, on opposite ends of the table, should each start off with a shot glass and a quarter.

Play

Both players start at the same time--each trying to bounce a quarter into their respective shot glasses as quickly as possible. Once a player is successful then he passes the shot glass and quarter to the next person. A shot glass cannot be passed until the player lands the quarter into it. A starting player must pass his glass to the right if it takes him more than one bounce to get the quarter into the glass. If a starting player is successful on the first bounce, then he passes the glass and quarter to the player on his left. The next player then has to bounce the quarter into the shot glass. If this player is successful on the first try then she passes the glass back to the person who passed it to her. If it takes more than one try, then the shot glass and quarter are passed in the same direction.

A player has to drink five drinks when she ends up with both shot glasses in front of her. After this happens, the round is over. The person who drinks and the player opposite her are the ones who start the next round.

DIME TOSS

Number of Players 2+

Setup

Partially fill several cups, shot glasses, and mugs with various drinks. They should be placed together on one side of a table (or on the floor). All players should be of equal distance from the arrangement of beverages, however, the distance selected can vary depending on the players' dime tossing abilities. It is recommended that players stand at least five feet away from the beverages. Each player should be equipped with several dimes (or other change).

Play

Players take turns tossing dimes into the containers--in the same manner as one would do at a carnival dime toss booth. When a player lands a dime into one of the containers, he can then assign another player to drink the entire drink in that container (or a replacement beverage if the drinker does not want a drink that contains dime grime). The game ends when all of the drinks in the playing area have been consumed.

CARD GAMES

ASSHOLE

Number of Players 3 - 8

Setup

Begin by dealing clockwise until the entire deck has been dealt out (some players may have one card more than others).

Ranking

2s are the highest card and are considered wild. The rest of the cards rank in this order (from highest to lowest): A, K, Q, J, 10, 9, 8, 7, 6, 5, 4, 3.

Play

The object of the game is to run out of cards before the other players. Players are assigned positions based on the order in which they run out of cards. After rank is established, a player may assign drinks to other players.

For the first round only, the person to the left of the dealer initiates the first round of play. This person may play either a one, two, three, or four card group (which only contains cards of the same rank). The initiator of a round establishes the group number for that round. For example, if the first person plays a pair of 4s then only pairs can be played during the course of the round. The next player has to match what the first player lays down, play something higher, or pass. If he plays a card (or pair of cards) of the same rank then the next player is skipped. A player may pass even if she has a play. When a player passes, she can not play again until the next round.

A person cannot play a group that contains more cards than the previous play (unless he is starting a new round). For example, if the initiator of the round plays three 4s, the second person must play three 5s or higher. Likewise, a player cannot play a group that contains fewer cards than the previous play (unless he is starting a new round). The 2s are the only exception to this rule. A player can lay down a single 2 during his turn, which immediately ends the round. Even if the round is being played with groups of three or four, only one 2 is necessary to end the round.

A round ends when all of the players (except one) have passed, or a two is played. The one who did not pass or who played the two in the previous round initiates the next round. At this point, the cards from the previous round are swept from the playing area and the one who starts the new round is able to lead with one, two, three, or four of a kind. Again, the first play determines the group size that may be played during the round.

Once a player runs out of cards then she is assigned a position and the other players continue playing until only one player is left with cards.

Positions

The person who runs out of cards first earns the rank of president, the second person is the vice president, and the last person is the asshole. For games with more than three players, additional ranks can be added such as: secretary, treasurer, business manager, and vice asshole.

Drinking

A player who ranks higher than another can assign drinks to that person at any time, for any reason. The president can assign drinks to anyone at the table, the vice president can assign drinks to everyone except the president, and the asshole cannot assign drinks to anyone. The president is also able to make up whatever rules she wants as long as the violation of the rule results in a drink assignment (see Appendix A for sample rules).

Continued Play

Once positions are established, a few rules should be added, unless the president vetoes them. The asshole is the one who has to deal. He deals to himself first, then deals from the lower to the higher ranks. Since the entire deck is dealt out, the lower ranking players are the ones who get stuck with any extra cards. The asshole is also the one who has to sweep the cards at the end of each round.

Before the first round of the game begins, the president may make the asshole trade her best two cards with him. In exchange, the president can give the asshole whatever two cards she chooses. In a game with four players or more, the vice president can force the second lowest ranking player to give up his best card in exchange for whatever card the vice president wants to un-load.

Once positions are established, the order of play becomes based on rankings. The president starts off the first round, followed by the vice president, and so on. The asshole plays last during the first round. Ranking does not change until the end of the game. Even if a low ranking player plays all of her cards before the president, the president may still assign drinks to that person until only one player has cards left.

BIG TWO

Number of Players 3 - 8

Ranking

The different suits are ranked, from highest to lowest, as follows: ♠, ♥, ♦, ♣.

Play

Played the same way as Asshole, except now the acceptable plays for a round include one of a kinds, two of a kinds, and poker hands. A poker hand must contain five cards--three of a kinds, two pairs, and four of a kinds are not acceptable plays. The acceptable poker hands are:

- Straight flush: five consecutive cards in the same suit
- Full house: three cards of one rank, two cards of another
- Flush: five cards of the same suit
- Straight: five consecutive cards of any suit

When a poker hand is led at the start of the round, other players may only play poker hands of the same type and each play must be higher than the previous one. A straight with the same numbers can be played if the highest number of the straight is of a higher suit than the previous player's straight. Also, only a flush containing higher numbers or a higher ranking suit may be played on a flush.

2s are not wild but they are still the highest card. Solitary 2s can only be played when singles are played during the round; a pair of 2s must be played for a round of pairs. A 2 does not end the round unless other players do not play a 2 of a higher suit and everyone passes.

Drinking

Same rules as Asshole. A player must drink when he is told to by a higher ranking officer or when he breaks one of the rules.

SUPER ASSHOLE

Number of Players 3 - 8

Play

Played the same as Big Two except with more poker combinations. Acquaint yourself with the rules of Asshole and Big 2 before attempting to play this game. Straights and flushes can contain anywhere from two to thirteen cards. Also, three of a kinds, four of a kinds, and consecutive pairs are allowed. Consecutive pairs can include any number of pairs. As with Big Two and Asshole, once a certain play is led, the other players follow by laying down a higher ranking play of the same group number, the same number of consecutive pairs, or the same poker hand type. Their plays must contain the same number of cards. For example, if a straight of three cards is played, then the next player can only play a higher three-card straight, or a three-card straight with the same face values in a higher ranking suit.

Drinking

Same rules as Asshole. A player must drink when she is told to by a higher ranking officer or when she breaks one of the rules.

MORE CARD GAMES

ROYALTY

Number of Players 2 - 6

Setup

Remove the cards with the face values of 2 through 7 from the deck. Then spread out the remaining cards on the playing area. They must be face down.

Card Values

The cards take on the following rank from highest to lowest: A, K, Q, J, 10, 9, 8. Pairs rank higher than non-pairs. Sequences and royalty card combinations do not have a higher ranking than non-specialty card combinations.

Play

Each player takes two cards from the pile and places them face down in front of him or her. The player who earned the lead from the previous round flips his cards over first. If it is the first round, then the player on the left of the dealer flips her cards over first. The following actions should be taken for the specified combinations:

- A pair (two cards of the same rank): the player makes a rule. The rule can be anything that limits how all the players act or speak during the game (see Appendix A for sample rules). Anyone who violates the rule must take a drink.

- A sequence (two cards with sequential ranking): a player can assign two drinks to any player.

- Q & J (any suit): the player can assign any number of drinks to another player but also has to drink the same number.

- K & J (any suit): the player must choose another card. The number that he chooses corresponds to the number of drinks that he has to take. Number cards are worth two drinks and face cards are worth four. If he draws an ace then he does not have to drink. He can then tell another player to draw and drink the number of drinks corresponding to the card she selects. If that player then chooses an ace then she can tell him to drink as many drinks as she chooses.

- K & Q (any suit): all other players must take three drinks.

If the player does not have any of these combinations then no drinks are assigned. The next person in order then flips his cards over. After all of the cards are flipped over, the player who has the highest ranking cards becomes the leader for the next round. If two players tie for the highest ranking cards, then the one who turned his cards over first starts the next round. To celebrate the end of the round, all players must take a social drink (except the new leader).

FOUR KINGS

Number of Players 3+

Setup

Remove all of the cards with the values of 2 through 8 from the deck. Place a large cup in the center of the table and spread out the remaining cards face down around it.

Play

The loser of the last round or the selected leader (for the first round) begins by choosing a card from the pile. She must then carry out an action based on the value of the card selected. Players continue drawing cards and carrying out the necessary actions. The six possible actions are:

A: the player to the left must take a drink.

Q: a category must be played.

J: the player to the right must take a drink.

10: a category must be played.

9: the player who selected the card must take a drink.

K: if the card chosen is the first, second, or third king the player pours some of her drink into the center cup. The one who draws the last king drinks the center cup.

Categories

When a player draws a Q or a 10 he must come up with a category topic. He must then list one of the items that fits into that category. Examples of topics include: types of footwear, comic strip characters, sports teams, etc. The next player then has three seconds to name something that fits into this category. The players continue naming items until someone gives a bad answer. Possible bad answers are:

- A repeated item
- An item that does not fit into the category
- A response that took longer than three seconds

The player who gives a bad answer has to take a drink.

The game ends after a player draws the fourth king and finishes drinking the center drink.

DRINKING HEARTS

Number of Players 2 - 8

Setup

If necessary, remove a few of the low cards from the deck, so that each player will be dealt the same number of cards. For example, if there are five players remove two low cards so that each player will receive ten cards. Remove cards in this order: 2♣, 2♦, 2♠, 3♣, etc. Do not remove any of the hearts. Players should set the drink penalty before the first game begins.

Ranking

In each suit the highest ranking card is the A, followed by K, Q, J, 10, 9, 8, 7, 6, 5, 4, 3, 2.

Play

Deal out the entire deck. Before play begins, players have the opportunity to get rid of unwanted cards. If there are two to four players, each person must pass three cards of his or her choice. Only two cards should be passed if there are more than four players. The recipient of the passed cards changes with each round. At the start of the first round, pass cards to the person on your left. During the second round pass your cards to the person on your right. On the third round, pass to the person who is two to the left, etc. Continue passing in this rotation until everyone passes to the person directly across from them. The following round does not have a pass, then the passing rotation repeats.

The person with the lowest club leads the first play. All players must follow suit if they are able to. If someone can't follow suit then she may play whatever card she chooses. Hearts must be broken (played on a non-heart lead) before one can be led; if the Q♠ is played before any hearts, then hearts are considered to be broken. The player who played the highest card of the suit led must take the trick (a play that includes one card from each player) and subsequently leads the next one.

The object of the game is to avoid getting points. Each heart is worth one point, the Q♠ is worth 13 points, and the J♦ is worth -11 points. If a player gets all of the points then she "shoots the moon". Shooting the moon gives the player -26 points or -37 points with the J♦. The J♦ is not needed for shooting the moon but all other point cards are.

Drinking

At the end of the round (when all the cards have been played out) the players count the number of points contained in the tricks that they've taken. The player with the highest number of points has to take the penalty drinks before the next round ends. If the person does not finish the drinks by that time then the penalty doubles. Also, if a player shoots the moon then all of the other players must take the penalty drinks before the end of the next round.

DRINKING POKER

Number of Players 2 - 10

Setup

Each player draws a card from the deck. The person who flips over the highest ranking card deals first. If two or more players tie (with the highest cards), then they must each draw another card. Then, the highest ranking card of the second draw wins the first deal. Each player is dealt five cards.

Card Ranking

The cards are ranked in the following order, from highest to lowest: A, K, Q, J, 10, 9, 8, 7, 6, 5, 4, 3, 2. The A can also be used as a 1 if it is used in the straight 5-4-3-2-A (which is the second highest straight after A-K-Q-J-10). Jokers, if you include them in the deck, are used as wild cards.

Ranking of Hands

The ranking of the hands, from highest to lowest, is as follows:

- Five of a kind: four cards of the same rank and a joker
- Royal flush: the highest ranking straight flush (A-K-Q-J-10)
- Straight flush: five sequentially ranked cards in the same suit
- Four of a kind: four cards of the same rank
- Full house: three cards of one rank and two cards of another
- Flush: five cards of the same suit
- Straight: five cards ranked sequentially--different suits.
- Three of a kind: three cards of the same rank
- Two pair: two cards of one rank and two cards of another
- One pair: two cards of the same rank

Within each ranking, hands containing higher value cards beat hands of the same rank that contain lower value cards. For example: The straight A-K-Q-J-10 ranks higher than the straight J-10-9-8-7.

The joker can take on another card's value to complete a hand. If none of the players have any of the above hands, then the one with the highest ranking cards wins.

Betting

Players bet drinks if they think they can pull the highest hand. The dealer calls an ante (a starting bet) before anyone looks at their cards. If a player accepts cards, then she must be in for the ante.

There are two rounds of betting: one before the draw and one after the draw. The first player to the dealer's left (who is still in the game) starts each round of betting. He has three options: betting a number of drinks, passing (betting zero drinks), or folding (dropping out of the hand). When a player folds, he places his cards face down on the table. The next player has to either match the bet, raise it, fold or pass. A player can only pass if the previous player passed.

The betting round ends after all players have either bet or folded. Anyone who folds before the first round of betting must drink the ante amount. If a player folds during or after a betting round then he must drink the amount of the bet that he had previously wagered.

Players can set a limit on the number of wagered drinks for individual bets and on the number of raises allowed.

Drawing Cards

Players who do not fold can draw cards between the two rounds of betting. Each player can draw a maximum of three cards unless she would like to draw four cards to an ace. If the player is drawing four cards to an ace, then she must show the ace to the other players.

Winning the Hand

After the second round of betting, the remaining players take part in a "showdown." At this point, the players turn their cards over and the player who has the highest ranking hand wins. The losers of the showdown take the number of drinks corresponding to the final wager.

Variations

One simple variation is for the dealer to name a wild, such as 2s. The game would be played the same, except now, the specified wild card is used the same way that the jokers are used.

Another variation is to play for the lowest ranking hand. This version follows the same rules as mentioned above, only the players bet on who has the lowest ranking hand.

MATCH MAKING

Number of Players 2 - 6

Setup

Remove either all of the red cards or all of the black cards from the deck.

Place the remaining cards face down in the center of the playing area. Arrange the cards into rows and columns, so that they do not overlap each other.

Play

Players take turns trying to make matches: two cards with the same face value. For example, the 2♦ matches the 2♥.

A player starts a turn by flipping over one of the cards in the playing area. Then he must select another card and flip it over. If the cards don't match then he should turn both cards back over to their original positions. If they do match then he can assign a drink to one of the other players. After assigning a drink, then he can attempt to make another match. A turn ends when a player is unable to make a match. Successfully matched cards should be removed from the playing area.

A player is not allowed to turn over more than two cards at a time. If, at any point during the game, a player makes the mistake of turning over extra cards then he must take two drinks. The game ends when all 13 matches have been made.

Strategy Hints

To do well at this game, you should try to remember where each specific card is placed when it is first turned over. Then, when you stumble upon its match later in the game, you won't have to guess where you saw the first card. One way that you can aid your memory is by trying to make an association between the card's value and its position. For example, if you want to remember where the 3♦ is, check to see if it is the third card from any of the playing field edges. For larger numbered cards, it may be easier to think of simple math calculations. For example, if the 10♠ is in the second column and is the fifth card from the left you should remember (2 x 5 = 10).

MATCH MAKING WITH LAND MINES

Number of Players 2 - 6

Play

This game is set up and played the same way as Match Making. Familiarize yourself with the rules for Match Making before you continue. The jokers are added to the game to provide more variety and a little more drinking. The joker is a wild card that can be used to represent any card value in any suit. When a player selects a joker as her first card then she can select any other card as its match. If she selects a joker for the second card then it must be used as the match for the first card. When this happens, the player may assign three drinks to another player (instead of only one for a normal match).

When a match is made with a joker, place the cards face up at the side of the playing field. When a player turns over the card that the joker was used in place of, then he has hit a "land mine." The player must take three drinks and his turn ends. Remove the land mine card from the playing area. This card, the joker and the land mine's match should then be flipped over and placed with the other matches. The game ends after all 13 matches have been made.

EVEN MORE CARD GAMES

DRINK THE DIFFERENCE  +

Number of Players 2

Card Values

The cards have the following point values:

- A: 14
- K: 13
- Q: 12
- J: 11
- Numbered cards are worth their face values.

Setup

Deal each player five cards.

Play

Players select a card from their hand and place it face down on the table. Then both players flip their cards over. The player with the lowest card should drink the difference between the two cards. For example, if one player flips over a Q and the other has a 7, the one who played the 7 must drink five drinks (12 - 7 = 5).

Each round consists of five plays (one for each card in the players' hands). Players can't draw and must play all five of their cards during a round.

SMOKE OR FIRE

Number of Players 2

Setup

One player is the designated dealer and the other is the guesser.

Play

The guesser has to guess whether or not the card is a fire card (red) or a smoke card (black) before the dealer flips it over.

Drinking

If the guesser guesses incorrectly, then she must take a drink.

Continued Play

The dealer continues flipping over cards until he reaches the end of the deck--or until the guesser gets tired of drinking.

Variation

Have the dealer drink if the guesser guesses correctly.

IDIOT'S POKER

Number of Players 2+

Ranking

From highest to lowest: A, K, Q, J, 10, 9, 8, 7, 6, 5, 4, 3, 2.

Setup

Deal each player one card.

Play

Each player takes the card and sticks it to his forehead without looking at it (it may stick if a player hasn't washed his face for a few hours). The cards must be facing out so that the players can view each others' cards.

Betting

A player bets drinks based on whether or not he believes that his card is higher than everyone else's. The person to the left of the dealer initiates the betting. After she bets a certain number of drinks or passes (bets 0), then the next player can fold, call (be in for the same number of drinks), or raise the bet. If the player folds without having previously made a bet in the round, then she must take one drink (for the ante). If the player raises, then the number she wagers becomes the number of drinks that all the players must take if they stay in the game and lose. The bet continues around the table until all players either fold or agree to stay in the game for the number of drinks

40

stated in the most recent raise (or the original bet if no one raised the wager). If a player has placed a bet and wants to fold after a subsequent raise then he must take the number of drinks that he originally wagered.

Drinking

After betting ends, all players who are still in the game remove the cards from their foreheads and place them face-up on the table. The player with the highest ranking card wins. If there is a tie for the highest card, then all players in the tie win. The losers must take the number of drinks corresponding to the wager.

DRINK UP!!

 +

Number of Players 2

Setup

One player is the designated dealer, the other is the designated drinker. The dealer deals out ten cards to start off the first round of the game.

Card Values

- A: 4
- K: 3
- Q: 2
- J: 1

41

Play

The dealer flips over the cards one at a time and the drinker must immediately drink the number of drinks that corresponds to the card values assigned to the A, K, Q, and J. For example, if a K is turned over then the drinker must take three drinks.

The dealer must separate the played cards into two discard piles: one for non-drinking cards and the other for the drinking cards (As, Ks, Qs, and Js).

Once the dealer has flipped over the entire stack, he adds up the number of points in the drinking cards discard pile. This number is used to determine the number of cards dealt in the next round. Continue playing until the drinker completes a round without having any drinks assigned to her. The cards do not need to be shuffled between rounds.

Fool Your Friends

The nature of this game allows for the dealer to play a mean trick on an unsuspecting drinker. Switch the deck to a pinochle deck, without letting the drinker know about it.   Pinochle decks only contain 9s - As, which usually creates a game that never ends.

THIRTY-ONE

Number of Players 2 - 7

Setup

Each player places three shot glasses containing a beverage in front of him--cups filled with 1-2 ounces of the drink can be used if there is a shortage of shot glasses. To determine the first dealer, players draw cards. The person with the lowest card deals first. He deals three cards to each player and places the remainder of the deck in the middle of the playing area. Then the dealer should flip over one card to start a discard pile.

Card Values

- A: 11
- Face cards: 10
- Numbered cards are worth their face values.

Play

The player to the left of the dealer starts by either choosing the card on the top of the discard pile or by choosing the top card from the deck. She must then place one of her cards on the discard pile. Play continues clockwise until a player either knocks or draws a blitz (explained later).

Knocking

A player knocks on the table, instead of taking a turn, when he wants the round to be over. Each of the other players then has one last turn. Everyone must turn over their cards when the turn comes back to the one who knocked (the knocker cannot take another turn). The player with the lowest hand value must move one of her shot glasses to the "stockpile" (an edge of the playing area). If there is a tie for the lowest hand, then the tied players each lose a shot glass.

Blitz

If at any point in the round, a player gets a 31 (an A and two face cards of the same suit) then he should flip over his cards immediately. This ends the round and all of the other players lose a shot glass.

The End of the Deck

During the course of a round, the players may run out of cards in the draw pile. If this happens, take the top card off the discard pile and use it as the start of a new discard pile. Turn over the rest of the discard pile and make it the new draw pile (do not shuffle).

Continued Play

After a player loses all three shot glasses, she is allowed to play until she loses once more. Once a player loses four times then she is out of the game and can no longer be dealt cards.

If only two players remain, they are tied in points, and neither have shot glasses remaining in front of them, then the player with the highest ranking card wins. As are higher than face cards, face cards and tens do **not** outrank each other, and higher numbered cards outrank lower ones. If both players have the same high card then the player with the second highest ranking card wins. If the players have identical hands then the round is considered void and another round must be played.

The player who doesn't lose four times is the winner.

Drinking

Once the game has ended, everyone (except the winner) must take three shot glasses from the stockpile. When the winner gives the word, the losers must drink their shots as quickly as they can. The one who finishes last must drink the contents of the remaining three shot glasses. The winner determines who finishes last if there is any dispute. The player who drinks the extra three shots at the end of the previous game deals the first round of the next game.

Variation

An additional rule is to have anyone who knocks be required to put two shot glasses in the stockpile if she loses to all of the other hands. This rule also allows players to hold onto 31s until the end of the game, instead of being required to show them.

FOLLOW THE JACK

Number of Players 2 - 8

Play

Deal all cards face up. The dealer deals until he flips over a J. Then he deals one more card, which becomes the drink card. All players who have a card with the same value as the drink card must take the number of drinks corresponding to the value associated with the J. The drink card following the first J is worth one drink, the card following the second J is worth two, the card following the third is worth three, and the card following the fourth is worth four. The dealer does not resume dealing until all players have taken their drinks. If a J follows a J then the second J is considered the first drink card and the card following the second J is the next drink card.

The game ends after all drinks have been taken for the fourth drink card.

CUT FOR IT

Number of Players 2

Play

The first player cuts a deck of cards and flips over the new top card. He then passes the rest of the deck to the second player. The second player then cuts the deck and flips over the new top card. The two players then compare their cards and the player with the lowest card takes a drink.

The cards do not need to be reshuffled after each round. The loser of the previous round should be allowed the first cut. Also a cut must leave at least ten cards in both sections of the deck.

UP THE RIVER, DOWN THE RIVER

Number of Players 2 - 9

Setup

Deal each player four cards. Place eight cards face down in two lines of four. The top four cards represent the trip "up the river" and the bottom four correspond to the trip "down the river."

Play

The dealer starts the game by flipping over the first up the river card. Any player who has a card in his hand that matches this card has to place it on top of the up the river card and take a drink. If the player has two cards that match, then he must take two drinks. The number of drinks increases as the group continues up the river. If the player has a match for the second card then he must take two drinks. Three drinks are taken for each card matching the third and four drinks for each card matching the fourth.

After drinks are taken for the fourth up the river card, the dealer turns over the card in the fourth position in the down the river row. When players match down the river cards, they get to assign drinks to other players. The drink assignment can be split up between two or more players. The first card turned over allows for four drinks to be assigned for each match. The next card (the third down the river card) allows for three drinks to be assigned, then two for the next, and one for the last.

The round ends after all eight cards have been turned over and players have taken their assigned drinks. The cards should be collected and reshuffled before starting a new round.

Holding Plays

If a player is caught holding a card that is supposed to be laid down as a match, then she must finish her drink. If her drink is less than half full, it should first be refilled before she drinks it.

TRUMPSTER

Number of Players 4

Setup

Play the game with two teams of two. The team members should sit opposite each other. Players draw cards to determine the first dealer. The person who draws the highest card assigns the first deal to the player of his choice. The deal rotates clockwise for subsequent rounds. Deal each player six cards.

Ranking

Cards are ranked, from highest to lowest, in the following order: A, K, Q, J, 10, 9, 8, 7, 6, 5, 4, 3, 2.

Card Values

Only the top five cards have value; which are as follows:

A: 4

K: 3

Q: 2

J: 1

10: 5

Suit Ranking

For betting purposes, suits take on the following rank (from highest to lowest): ♠, ♥, ♦, ♣.

Determining Trump

Players wager drinks in order to determine who calls trump. When calling out a bet, the player states the number of drinks that he is willing to take and names the desired trump suit. The next player then places a bet that is either the same number of drinks and a higher ranking suit or a higher number of drinks for any suit. If the player does not want to bet higher, then he can pass. Once a player passes then he cannot bet again until the next round. After three players pass, trump becomes the suit that was called by the last bettor. Whoever placed the bet must take all of the drinks for the bet before play begins. His teammate is not allowed to help with the drinking.

Play

The opponent to the left of the dealer makes the opening play, which cannot be trump if she has non-trump cards. Players must follow suit if they are able to. If the player can't, then she may play trump or any other suit. The highest trump card takes the trick. If no trump cards are played then the highest ranked card of the suit led takes it. The player who takes the trick leads the next one. Trump cannot be led until it has been broken (played on a non-trump lead). The only exception to this rule is when the leader only has trump cards to choose from.

Drinking

After all six tricks are played, each team must count the number of points in the tricks that they took. Then calculate the difference between the two teams totals. The team with the lower number of points loses. If the losing team did not call trump, then the total number of drinks that the team must take is equal to the difference between the teams' totals. If the losing team was the team that called trump, then they must drink double the difference of the totals. The two team members may divide up the total number of drinks any way they choose.

TRUMPSTER II

Number of Players 4

Setup

Players draw cards to determine the first dealer. The person who draws the highest card gets to assign the first deal to the player of his choice.

Play the game with two teams of two. The team members should sit opposite each other. Deal each player six cards.

Ranking

Cards are ranked, from highest to lowest, in the following order: A, K, Q, J, 10, 9, 8, 7, 6, 5, 4, 3, 2.

Suit Ranking

For betting purposes, suits take on the following rank, from highest to lowest: ♠, ♥, ♦, ♣.

Card Values

Only the top five cards have value, which are as follows:

A: 4

K: 3

Q: 2

J: 1

10: 5

Object

The object of Trumpster II is different than Trumpster. In this game, the team that calls trump wants to obtain the **exact** number of points corresponding to the bet that one of their team members places.

Determining Trump

To determine trump, players bet the number of total points that they think their teams can take in the game. When calling out a bet, the player must state the number of points that she thinks her team can take and name her desired trump suit. Players are not allowed to consult their partners when placing a bet. If the next player places a bet, it must be for the same number of points and a higher ranking suit or for a higher number of points and any suit. If the player does not want to bet higher then she must pass. Once a player passes, she cannot bet again until the next game. After three players have passed, trump becomes the suit that was called by the last bettor.

Play

The opponent to the left of the dealer makes the opening play (which cannot be trump if the player has non-trump cards). Players must follow suit if they are able to. If a player cannot, then he may play trump or any other suit. The highest trump card takes the trick; if no trump cards are played then the highest card of the suit led takes it. The player who takes the trick leads the next one. Trump cannot be led until it has been broken (played on a non-trump lead). The only exception to this rule is when the leader only has trump cards to choose from.

Drinking

After all of the six tricks have been played, then the teams count the number of points in the tricks that they took. If the team that called the trump suit gets the same number of points that they had wagered, then each member of the other team must take a drink for each point of the wager. If the team that called trump made their bid and obtained more points than they wagered then both teams will end up drinking. Each member of the other team will have to take a drink for each point of the wager. Each member of the team that called trump will have to take a drink for each point taken that was greater than the wager. For example, if Team A bet 7 and pulled 10 tricks, then each member of Team B drinks 7 and each member of Team A drinks 3. If the team that placed the bet got fewer points than what they bet, then each member of that team must take the number of drinks corresponding to the wager.

DIE GAMES

FIVE DIE ROLL

Number of Players 2+

Setup

Five dice are needed.

Play

Five die roll is similar to five card draw poker. Players get two rolls to make different dice combinations. After making the first roll, the player must keep and set aside at least one die. The player should then roll the remaining dice again.

Drinking

If a player does not make a combination during his turn then he must take a drink and pass the dice. If a player has one of these rolls then he can assign the following number of drinks:

- Five of a kind (all five dice are the same number)   10 drinks
- Four of a kind (four of the dice are the same number)   6 drinks
- Full house (three of one number, two of another)   5 drinks
- Straight (five consecutive numbers)   3 drinks
- Three of a kind (three of the dice are the same number) 1 drink

Drink assignments can be split between players.

If the player makes one of these combinations then she takes another turn. The player can continue taking turns until she does not get one of the combinations. Once a player has a bad roll, she must take a drink and pass the dice.

FIVE DIE ROLL-TWO'S WILD

Number of Players 2+

Play

Played the same as five die roll only now the two is considered to be wild. If you haven't done so already, read the rules for Five Die Roll before continuing with this section. If one of the following combinations is rolled then the corresponding number of drinks can be assigned:

- Five twos (all five dice are twos)   15 drinks
- Five of a kind (all five dice are the same number)   8 drinks
- Four of a kind (four of the dice are the same number) 5 drinks
- Full house (three of one number, two of another)   3 drinks
- Straight (five consecutive numbers)   1 drink

A two can be used as any other number or as itself (for straights). Three of a kinds are not worth anything in this version.

THREE-MAN

Number of Players 2+

Setup

Use two dice. First, the players should be asked if someone is willing to be the three-man. Then each player rolls both dice and the highest number goes first. If no one had previously volunteered to be the three-man then the person who had rolled the lowest number is designated as the three-man.

Play

At the start of a player's turn, he rolls the dice and tries to get one of the "good" rolls. Each of the good rolls listed below has an associated action that must be taken immediately following the roll:

- 7: The person to the left of the roller drinks.
- 11: The person to the right of the roller drinks.
- 3 on one die: The three-man takes one drink.
- Doubles: Pass both dice to one or two other players. The number they roll tells them how much to drink. If a player rolls a 1 on one of the dice, then he returns the die to the initial roller and she must roll it again. She must then drink double the number that is showing on the die unless she rolls a 1, then she gives the die back to the other player for triple the amount rolled, and so on.

- Double 3s: The three man takes two drinks and the roller can pass the dice to one or two of the other players (the same rules apply as the "ones" rule under Doubles).

After making one of the good rolls, the player can roll again. If the player did not make a good roll, then the dice must be passed to the next player.

Changing the Three-Man

The three-man will continue to drink whenever someone rolls a three until he rolls a three. When he does this, he can assign any player to be the new three-man. If the three-man does not roll a three during his turn then he must continue as the three-man for at least one more full round. If the three-man rolls double threes during his turn, he can appoint two three-men or can make one player be the double three-man. A double three-man has to drink two drinks every time a three is rolled.

In order to reduce the number of three-men back to one person (when there are two three-men), one of the existing three-men must roll a three and appoint the other three-man as the double three-man. When a double three-man rolls a three, she appoints another player as a three-man (not a double three-man). However, if the double three-man rolls double threes then everyone must chug an entire drink, and the double three-man gets to appoint another double three-man.

ASSEMBLY LINE

Number of Players 3+

Setup

Use three dice. Several communal drinks should be poured and placed in the center of the table. The communal drinks should be reserved for the assembly lines. In addition, each player should have his own drink.

Play

Players take turns rolling the dice. Each player is only allowed one roll per turn. Once the player takes her turn, and any necessary drinking has been done, she passes the dice to the person on her left.

Drinking

When a player makes one of the following rolls, the corresponding drinking activity must occur:

- All even numbers: the player to the left of the roller must take a drink.
- All odd numbers: the player to the right of the roller must take a drink.
- Three of a kind (except three sixes): the roller may tell one of the other players to finish his drink.

- Three sixes: the roller must finish his drink.
- Straight (three consecutive numbers): carry out an assembly line.

Assembly Line

The player who rolls the straight initiates the assembly line. She must take one of the drinks from the center of the table and then drink as much as she wants from the cup. She can take only a small sip or may drink the entire drink. She must then pass the cup to the person on her left, who then drinks as much as he wants. The cup is passed from player to player until it reaches the last person in the assembly line (seated to the right of the roller). Each player must take at least take one drink from the cup unless the drink has already been consumed by the time it reaches him or her. The last person has to finish the drink. Only empty cups can come off the end of the assembly line.

MEXICALI

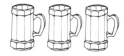

Number of Players 3+

Setup

Players need to be seated around a smooth surfaced table. The game requires a non-transparent cup and two dice. The dice must be placed underneath the cup.

Ranking

Die combinations take on the following rank from highest to lowest:

- Specialty rolls: Mexicali (21), Reverse (42), Thumb Rule (41) and Social (31). All specialty rolls have the same rank (the drink assignments are explained later).
- Doubles: within the doubles category, the possible combinations have the following rank from highest to lowest: 66, 55, 44, 33, 22, 11.
- All other rolls: rolls that do not count as a specialty roll or as doubles have a lower rank. Rolls within this category are ranked based on their actual value: 65 is the highest possible roll in this category and 32 is the lowest.

Play

The first player starts the round by shaking the cup (thereby rolling the dice). The player then tilts the cup so that only he can view the outcome of the roll. To determine the actual number of the roll, the player takes the highest number of the two dice and uses it as the first digit of the actual number and the lower die value becomes the second digit. For example, if the player rolls a five and a three, then the actual number is a 53 (not a 35). The player can bluff by announcing a number that is not the same as what he rolled. After calling a number, the player then slides the cup to the next player. When sliding the cup, players must make sure that the dice are not accidentally rerolled.

The next player then has two options:

1) Roll the dice. The player must reroll the dice and tilt the cup so that only she can view the outcome of the roll. The player then has to announce a number that is of higher or equal rank (only allowed for specialty rolls). If the player's roll is lower in rank, she must either bluff or drink automatically and pass the cup to the player on her left. If the player calls a number then the next player will then be faced with the same two options. If she decides to take a drink then the next player starts off a new round.

2) Accuse the player of bluffing. To call a bluff the player lifts up the cup. If the previous player had lied about his roll then he must take a drink. The accuser then starts a new round. If the previous player didn't lie then the person who called the bluff must take a drink. The dice return to the previous player and he starts a new round.

Specialty Rolls and Doubles

Besides when a bluff is called, there are two other instances when players must drink: when any player has rolled or has successfully bluffed a specialty or doubles roll. When a player claims to have one of these two types of dice combinations, action is not taken immediately (except with the Thumb Rule-explained later). Instead, after the player announces the roll then she slides the cup to the next player. This player then decides whether or not she thinks that the previous player is bluffing. If she decides not to call the bluff then the action associated with these rolls is carried out before she rolls. If she decides to lift up the cup then the action taken depends on the actual roll. If the previous player bluffed then he must take a drink and no other action is taken. If the previous player did not bluff then the person who called the bluff must take a drink. Then, the action associated with the roll is carried out.

Here's what you do if you make one of these rolls:

- Mexicali (21): the roller may pull the cup off of the dice on a Mexicali if he chooses to do so. He may then ask one or two other people to roll the dice. The player(s) must then drink the total number of drinks as shown by the dice. If a 1 is rolled, the die is returned to the initial roller and rerolled. The roller must then drink double the number shown unless a 1 is rolled again. If this occurs, then the die is passed back for triple drinks, and so on. If the roller passes the cup, the next player calls his bluff, and he does have a Mexicali, then the accuser must roll both dice and drink double the total. Any 1s rolled will be passed back to the initial roller and the total drinks is then four times the amount shown on the dice, and so on. If the initial roller rolls a 1 then the die is passed back to the accuser, and she faces drinking eight times the amount of the die's value if she does not roll a 1. Continue passing the dice back and forth and doubling the drink multiplier until a number other than a 1 is rolled.
- Reverse (42): If this is called then pass the dice in the opposite direction and reverse the order--unless a bluff is caught.
- The Thumb Rule (41): If this is rolled or bluffed the player does not state the number. Instead he places his right thumb on the table. When the other players notice, they must also place their right thumbs

on the table. The last player to do this has to drink (provided that the next player does not successfully catch the roller bluffing).

- Social (31): The roller lifts the cup and everyone takes a drink, or the cup is passed and everyone drinks. If a bluff is called and the roll is a 31, then the accusor must drink a full beverage and everyone else takes a social drink. If the roller lifts the cup then he starts a new round after the social drink.

Players should only drop out between rounds. The game ends when everyone decides to quit.

DOUBLES DARE

Number of Players 2+

Setup

Two dice are needed for this game. Each player should be given five strips of paper and a pen or pencil.

Each player thinks up five dares and writes each one down on a strip of paper (see Appendix D for sample dares). Everyone must fold their dares and place them in a bowl or hat. Players should not show or tell each other their dares. Before the dares are written, players may agree that certain types of dares are not allowed (e.g. those involving nudity).

Also, before starting the game, each player must select a number between one and six. The number chosen by the player will be that player's number for the entire game.

Play

The first player takes his turn by rolling the dice. There are four corresponding actions that must be taken for some of the possible dice combinations:

- Only one of the dice is the roller's number: the roller assigns a drink to another player.
- Doubles (of the roller's number): the player picks a dare from the bowl/hat. After reading the dare, the player has two choices: either to perform the dare or to drink five drinks. If carried out, the dare must be performed to the satisfaction of at least half of the other players.
- Doubles (of a number that isn't the roller's number): the roller chooses another player, who must select a dare. After reading the dare, the player has two choices: either to perform the dare or drink five drinks. If carried out, the dare must be performed to the satisfaction of the player who assigned it.
- All other rolls: if a player's roll does not fall into any of the three previously mentioned categories then he must take a drink.

Each player is only allowed one roll per turn. The player must wait for the action associated with the roll to be completed before he passes the dice to the next player.

The game ends when all of the dares have been carried out or discarded.

Discarding Dares

A dare may be thrown out if at least half of the players feel that the dare violates one of the previously determined dare type restriction rules.

Variation

Players could add an additional rule, which gives a player the option to perform a dare instead of rolling. The player must perform the dare and does not have the option to drink. After performing the dare, he can then assign someone to drink. That person then rolls a die and drinks the number of drinks corresponding to that roll. After she finishes drinking, then she passes the dice to the person whose turn falls after the player who performed the dare.

ENTERTAINMENT GAMES

DRAMATIC DRINKING

Number of Players 2+

Setup

A drama series should be playing on the television. You should watch an evening or daytime soap opera if you want to hit the drinking conditions more frequently.

Play

While watching the show, all the players must take a certain number of drinks when the characters perform certain actions.

Take one drink if:

- Two of the characters get in an argument.
- Two of the main characters are in bed together.
- Someone is jealous of another person's relationship.
- A passionate kiss is exchanged.
- Someone lies to get out of a tough predicament.
- One of the characters takes a drink.

Take three drinks if:

- One of the characters cheats on his/her significant other.

- Anyone goes to a party.

- One of the characters quits a job.

- Anyone loses a job.

- One character blackmails another.

- Someone goes on a vacation.

- The commercial break includes at least one ad for a product that is only used by women.

Take five drinks if:

- One of the regular cast members has a near death experience.

- One of the characters gets arrested.

- Someone's house or business catches on fire.

- Anyone is accused of murder.

- Two of the regular cast members hook up for the first time.

PICK A WORD

Number of Players 2 +

Setup

Players select a song or a set of songs to listen to (the radio may be used). Then each player must be assigned a word. A player may not select his own word, it must be assigned by one or by many of the other players.

Play

Start the music. When the player's word is sung then she must drink. Players drink each time their words are sung until the song/set of songs ends or the group decides to stop playing. The group may decide to change a player's word at any point in the game, as long as the majority of the group agrees to the change.

BOAT RACES

Number of Players 12 +

Setup

Players must divide themselves into teams of four. If there are players left over, then the extras can be alternates and can rotate into a team after each round.

Players determine which two teams will race first. The two teams line up on opposite sides of a table. The first person in line is the anchor. Each player must be equipped with a cup, the anchor must have two. The anchors are responsible for filling each cup with the selected beverage before the race begins. The amount consumed by each team member can vary but each member must have the same amount as the person opposite him or her.

Play

The two teams race to finish their five drinks first. The anchors start the race by drinking their beverages as fast as they can. After the team's anchor places his empty cup on the table, the second player in line starts chugging her beverage. This continues to the last person in line. Once the last person is done, the anchor drinks his second beverage. The team whose anchor finishes first wins the race. The losing team challenges the next team.

Disqualification

A team automatically loses if any one of its players:

- Spills more than a few drops of his beverage.
- Starts drinking before the previous team member has finished.
- Does not finish her beverage completely.

FOOTBALL MADNESS

Number of Players 2+

Setup

A television must be turned on and a football game must be starting or in progress. Before the drinking game begins, each player must announce the team that he is supporting.

Play

A player must take the corresponding number of drinks when the team that he is **not** rooting for does one of the following actions:

- First down: 1 drink
- Touchdown: 3 drinks
- Field goal: 1 drink
- Two-point conversion: 2 drinks
- Interception: finish your drink

A player must also take the corresponding number of drinks when the team that he is rooting for does one of the following:

- Fumble: 3 drinks
- Suffers a safety: 3 drinks

Variation

If most of the players intend to watch the commercials then you can add drinks that are based on the commercials. For example, you could have all players take a drink if a beverage is advertised. You can also have players take three drinks if the beverage that is advertised is the same type or brand that they are drinking.

WORD GAMES

PREPOSTEROUS PROPOSAL

Number of Players 2+

Setup

Each player must be given two identical looking pieces of paper. One piece should be marked with a 'Y' for yes and the other should be marked with an 'N' for no. Nothing should be written on the back sides of the papers. Players may substitute the pieces of paper with playing cards. A red suit could signify the "yes" card and a black suit could represent the "no" card.

Play

The first player starts the game by selecting another player to be the recipient. The first player then makes a "preposterous proposal" to him. The proposal has to be in the form of a yes/no question, such as, "Would you sleep with your mother's best friend for a million dollars?" (see Appendix B for more suggestions). Before the player responds, everyone else must first guess the answer. To venture their guesses, the other players must hold either the yes or no card in their right hands (in a manner that prevents others from seeing their guesses). The other card should be placed face down on the table or floor.

Once everyone is holding a card, the recipient of the proposal gives his answer. Then the other players show their cards to the group. Those who guessed incorrectly must take a drink.

The recipient of the previous proposal selects the next recipient and makes a preposterous proposal to her.

Variation

Have the recipient take three drinks if everyone else guesses the correct answer to the proposal. This serves as a punishment to that person for being so predictable.

I NEVER

Number of Players 2+

Play

Players take turns stating actions that they have never done. An example of an "I never" statement is, "I have never smoked a cigar." After a player states that she has not done something, every player who **has** carried out that action at least once before must take a drink. If a player makes a statement that she has not done something and no one else has done it either, then she must take a drink.

Catching Lies

A player must be honest when he states that he has never done something. If another person believes the player making the "I never" statement has actually done what he is claiming not to have done, then he can be accused of lying. In making this accusation the accuser must be able to support the claim by citing an instance when the accused had done the specified action. If the player is proved dishonest, he must drink five drinks.

TRUTH OR DRINK

Number of Players 2+

Setup

Players must set the number of drinks that are to be taken if a player does not wish to answer the question.

Play

One player begins by asking another player a personal question (for sample truth questions see Appendix C). That player can either answer the question honestly or drink the specified number of drinks. After the player answers or drinks then she can ask another player a personal question.

DRINK OR DARE

Number of Players 2+

Setup

Players must set the number of drinks that are to be taken if a player does not wish to do a dare.

Play

Played the same as Truth or Drink except, instead of asking personal questions, players dare each other (for sample dares see Appendix D). The recipient of the dare must perform it or drink the specified number of drinks.

Restricting Dares

At any point in the game, a player may question the appropriateness of a dare. If at least half of the players decide that the dare is inappropriate then it can be discarded. The darer must then think of another dare.

To avoid discarding many dares, players should discuss what is acceptable before starting the game. Then everyone can agree that certain types of dares cannot be asked (for example, dares involving nudity).

THUMPER

Number of Players 3+

Setup

Players must be seated around a table in a manner which allows them to place their hands at the edge of the table. Each person must choose a hand gesture that he would like to use during the game (i.e. thumbs up, waving, etc.). There are a few restrictions on the types of gestures that can be made. All players must be able to see the gesture when it is performed and all gestures must be unique (two players can not use the same gesture). Once the gestures are selected, they need to be performed a few times so everyone else at the table is aware of the other players' gestures.

Play

The person who leads a new round is the one who had erred in the previous round (or a volunteer, for the first round only). During the entire round everyone must be thumping the table with their hands, in a fashion similar to a drum roll. At the start of the round, the following dialogue must take place (once everyone has started thumping):

Leader: "What's the name of the game?"

Everyone Else: "Thumper."

Leader: "How do you play it?"

Everyone Else: "Thump like this."

Leader: "Why do we play it?"

Everyone Else: "To drink a lot."

All players must continue thumping. The initiator of the round passes the lead to someone else by lifting her hands off the table and performing her gesture once and then performing someone else's gesture once. The gestures must be performed in unison with everyone else's thumping. The person whose gesture was just performed now has the lead. The new leader then has only a few seconds before the lead has to be passed to someone else in a similar manner.

Ending a Round

The round ends when a player makes a mistake. A mistake can occur at any time in the round and includes the following:

- Mispronouncing the initial dialogue or not saying it at the right time
- Performing a gesture improperly
- Performing a gesture that does not belong to anyone
- Not performing your own gesture before performing another player's gesture.
- Tapping out of rhythm or ceasing to tap for a reason other than gesturing
- Gesturing when the lead belongs to someone else

Drinking

The one who makes the mistake and ends the round has to take a drink and must initiate the next round.

COLORS

Setup

Players must be seated in a circle. If you are at a table, you should back away from it. Each player must select a color to represent him. Each player should announce his color before the game is started so that everyone is aware of the colors that are being used in the game. A player may not use a color that has already been selected by another player. It is recommended that one-syllable color names be used.

Play

The person who leads a new round is the one who had erred in the previous round (or a volunteer, for the first round only). All players must maintain a rhythm throughout the entire round. The rhythm consists of repeatedly slapping one's thighs twice and then clapping twice. The leader is the one who sets the pace for the rhythm. He may speed up or slow down the pace and the other players must follow. The leader has to state his own color each time everyone slaps their thighs and then must state one of the player's colors each time everyone claps. If the leader states his own color again, then he keeps the lead. If he chooses a color that is not his own, then the lead is passed to the owner of the stated color. The new leader must then state her color when everyone slaps their thighs and then she is able to transfer the lead when everyone claps.

Ending the Round

The round ends when a mistake is made. The following is a list of the possible mistakes:

- The leader does not state her color twice during the two thigh slaps.
- The leader does not state a player's color twice during the clapping.
- Anyone slaps or claps out of rhythm.

Drinking

The one who ends the round must take a drink and must start the next round.

Options

Players may choose other categories (i.e. sex toys, sports teams, etc.).

SPIN THE BOTTLE

Number of Players 4+

Setup

Players sit in a circle and place a bottle in the center.

Play

A player spins the bottle and waits to see who the bottle points to. The spinner then has to either kiss that person on the lips or drink three drinks. The game can't continue until someone has been kissed or drinks have been taken. The person on the previous spinner's left spins the bottle next.

CATEGORIES

Number of Players 2+

Play

Players take turns coming up with category topics. The player who chooses a topic also names one item that fits into the category. Examples of topics are: types of footwear, comic strip characters, etc. The next player then has three seconds to name something that also fits into that category. The players continue naming items until someone gives a bad answer. Bad answers include:

- A repeated item
- An item that does not fit in the category
- A response that took longer than three seconds

The player who gives a bad answer has to take a drink.

CELEBRITIES

Number of Players 2+

Play

Players take turns naming celebrities. The celebrity's first name has to begin with the same first letter as the first letter of the last name of the celebrity named by the previous player. For example, if the first player says "Attila the Hun", then the next player has to think of a celebrity whose first name starts with an 'H'. If the player names a celebrity whose first and last names both start with the same letter, then the order is reversed. For example, if the second person in the previous example said "Henrietta Hefferstein", then the first person would now have to name a celebrity whose first name starts with 'H'.

Drinking

If a player names a celebrity that does not start with the correct letter, if the celebrity was already named, or if he takes too long to answer, he must take a drink. He must also take an additional drink for every ten seconds that he is unable to name an appropriate celebrity. After the third drink he may ask other players for assistance.

If no one else has heard of a named celebrity, then the player must come up with another name within ten seconds. If she is unable to do this then she must take two drinks. She may then ask the other players for assistance.

GEOGRAPHY

Number of Players 2+

Play

One of the players starts the game by stating a geographical location. The next player must state a location name that starts with the same first letter as the last letter of the place named by the previous player. For example, if the first player says "Arkansas", then the next player has to think of a location that starts with the letter 'S', such as Slovakia. If a player names a place with the same first and last letter, then the order is reversed. If the first person said "Arkansas" and the second person said "Sioux Falls", then the first person would now have to name another place that starts with an 'S'.

Drinking

If a player names a geographical location that does not start with the correct letter, or if he takes too long to answer then he must start drinking. The player must continue drinking until he is able to name a location that starts with the correct letter. He may stop drinking after the third drink and ask another player for assistance.

DRINK!

Number of Players 2+

Play

    This game should be the easiest to learn out of all the games contained in this book. The designated leader starts the game by telling someone to drink. Then she drinks and tells another player to drink, then he drinks, etc.

IF I COULD HAVE ANYTHING.....

Number of Players 2+

Setup

    Players need to be arranged in a circle, organized so that the order of play is obvious to everyone. Select one player to be the leader.

Play

    The leader starts the game by saying "If I could have anything I want I would choose..." The leader then needs to think of a noun (a person, place, thing, or idea) that starts with an 'A'. The noun needs to be said without hesitation. The next player, the person to the leader's left, then has to make the same statement "If I could have anything I want I would choose....". She then has to state the 'A' word that the leader stated and then must name a noun that starts with a 'B'. Players around the circle continue taking turns, each time adding a noun that starts with the next letter in the alphabet.

Drinking

A player must take a drink for any of the following reasons:

- Not stating the initial statement correctly
- Fumbling over or slurring a word
- Taking more than approximately five seconds to name someone else's noun
- Taking more than three seconds to name her own noun
- Stating a noun that does not match what was stated in a previous turn
- Naming a word that is not a noun
- Stating a noun, for his letter, that does not start with the correct letter

If a player can't remember a noun, then he must first take a drink before asking for help. He must then start over from the beginning. If the player messes up again then he may ask for the noun related to another letter and start over (after taking another drink).

Eliminating Players

A player can only make three mistakes during a turn, before her turn is forfeited. After that, she is out of the game and must finish her drink. The next player then takes his turn and must use the same letter that should have been stated at the end of the previous player's turn. The game ends when only one player remains. If players reach the end of the alphabet then they should start at the beginning of the alphabet again. At this point the turn would involve stating the first 26 nouns followed by the nouns from the second set of letters.

THREE WORDS

Number of Players 2 +

Play

Players take turns making cohesive sentences out of three assigned words. The words are determined by the player who had taken the previous turn. The player who assigns the words may either pull the words from her vocabulary or consult a dictionary. If she decides to use a dictionary then the words must be randomly selected; she should flip to a page and point to a word without looking. The assignee may immediately ask for a word's meaning and the assignor must offer a brief definition. Once the player knows all three meanings, then he has ten seconds to think of a sentence. He must then recite it to the group.

Drinking

A player has to drink if he:

- Takes longer than 10 seconds to think of a sentence

- Uses a word incorrectly (as judged by the other players)

- Pauses for more than a second when reciting a sentence

- Fails to incorporate all three words

- States a sentence that is judged to be grammatically incorrect

- Asks for a word's meaning after starting a sentence

A player may assign a drink to another player if he is able to include her name in the sentence. Players that are included in the sentence cannot judge the correct usage of the words or the player's grammar.

ROCK, SCISSORS, PAPER

Number of Players 2

Gestures

Three hand gestures are used in this game. One is the rock, which is indicated by the hand forming a fist. The second is scissors, which is indicated by extending the pointer and middle finger outward with the other fingers and the thumb folded into the palm. The third gesture is the paper, indicated by placing the hand flat with the palm down.

Play

Players start the round by first making a fist with their right hands. The right hand is held over the left hand, which is held flat with the palm facing up. Then both players must perform the lead-in to the gesture. The lead-in consists of two counts of each player dropping and lifting their right hands into and out of their left hands. When the right hand hits the left hand for the third time it should then be changed to the desired hand gesture. Both players must perform the lead-in in sync with each other so that the gestures are displayed at the same time.

If the players have each made different gestures then the one whose gesture is destroyed by the other's has to take a drink. The three gestures have the following relationships:

- Rock smashes the scissors
- Paper covers the rock
- Scissors cut the paper

If the players have made the same gesture, then the result is a tie. No drinks are taken for a tie.

PARLOR GAMES

DRINKING CHESS

Number of Players 2

Setup

Set up the same way as normal chess.

Play

Played the same way as normal chess. If necessary, players should refamiliarize themselves with the standard rules of chess.

Drinking

When a player loses a piece, she must take the number of drinks that correspond to the particular piece. The following values are recommended:

- Pawn: 1 drink
- Knight: 2 drinks
- Bishop: 2 drinks
- Rook: 2 drinks
- Queen: 3 drinks
- King: 4 drinks

When a player is able to advance a pawn to the opposite side of the board, two things happen. Not only is the player able to exchange the pawn for a more powerful piece, she can also tell the other player to take the number of drinks that correspond to the new piece.

The game ends when the king is checkmated or when one of the players is no longer able or willing to continue drinking.

Variation

Players may add a rule that a player takes two drinks when his king is in check.

DRINK PONG

Number of Players 2 - 4

Setup

Place five to ten cups of various beverages at one end of the table. They should be placed close to the edge that runs parallel to the net. The cups should be filled at least one-quarter full (in order to keep them from being easily knocked over). All players should stand at the opposite end of the table.

Play

Players take turns trying to land a ping-pong ball into one of the beverage cups. A player is only allowed one bounce per turn. When a player lands a ball into a drink, she can assign another player to drink that beverage (or a replacement beverage, if players do not want a drink that contains ping-pong ball grime).

There are two methods for bouncing the ping-pong ball:

Option 1--hitting it with a paddle. When using a paddle the player is allowed to bounce the ball on the table and then must hit it over the net. The ball cannot hit the player's side of the table before it goes over the net.

Option 2--throwing it. If a player decides to use this method, he must hold the ball between his thumb and pointer finger. When throwing the ball across the table, the player's hand cannot be more than a foot above the table. The ball cannot bounce on the player's side before it goes over the net.

With both methods, the ball cannot hit the net when it is bounced across the table. Also the ball must bounce on the opposite side of the table before it bounces into the cup.

If a player violates any of the rules and the ball lands in a cup, then he must drink the beverage. If a player violates a rule but the ball does not land in a cup then the turn ends and no penalty is given.

The game ends when all of the drinks on the table have been consumed.

REDEMPTION

Number of Players 2 - 6

Setup

This game requires a pool table. All fifteen balls must be racked (it does not matter how they are organized).

Breaking

The rules of this game do not apply to the break. If the player who breaks sinks at least one ball into a pocket, then he may take another turn.

Play

Players take turns trying to sink balls into pockets. Players must call all shots by specifying the pocket. Bank shots and combinations must also be called. After a player makes the first shot, she can assign one drink. If she makes a second shot in the same turn then she can assign two drinks, etc. A player's turn is over after she misses or scratches.

Shit Shots

If a player lands a ball into one of the pockets and the shot was called incorrectly then he has made a "shit shot" (slop shot). He is not able to assign drinks for this shot and he must try to make two more shots for redemption. He starts by wagering a certain number of drinks. If he calls both shots and makes both into the called pockets, then he can assign the drinks to other players. If he misses one of the redemption shots, then he must take the number of drinks that he wagered. If the redemption shot is also a shit shot, then he must drink double the amount of his wager. The player's turn ends after the redemption shot is attempted.

Scratching

If a player sinks the cue ball (scratches) then she has to be the recipient of all the drinks that the next player assigns during the course of his turn. The only time this rule does not apply is if the next player fails to make the redemption shots.

After a scratch, the next player can place the cue ball at any spot on the table.

The game ends when all of the balls have been sunk. The last person to make a shot is the one who gets to break at the start of the next game. The rest of the shooting order stays the same. In other words, the second shooter will be the same person who shot after the new breaker in the previous game.

APPENDIX A.   RULES

- Players can not say any words that start with the letter 'D.'

- No one may touch the table with any part of his body except when picking up the dice or cards.

- A television theme song must be sung by each player throughout the course of his or her turn.

- First and last names cannot be used.

- Players must address each other by proceeding each name with the title "Master."

- Players cannot touch their drinks with their right hands.

- Lick your index finger before rolling or drawing a card.

- Bark each time you pass the quarter or dice.

- Stand up and scream expletives before each turn.

- Place your left thumb on the table whenever you take a turn.

- Roll the quarter off your nose for your third turn.

- Run around the table before taking a drink.

- Players cannot use their hands to drink.

- Whenever I drink, everyone else drinks.

- Everyone else takes a social drink when a player finishes a beverage.

- Yell "Geronimo" before bouncing a quarter, rolling the dice, or drawing a card.

- Gargle each drink before swallowing.

- Belch after each drink.

- Everyone drinks if the quarter comes up heads.

- Spank yourself if you break a rule.

APPENDIX B.   PROPOSALS

- Would you wipe dog poop on your face for $500?

- Would you appear naked in a music video with your favorite band for $200?

- Would you shave off all your body hair for fifty free CDs?

- Would you spend the night in a cemetery for $50?

- Would you read the dictionary from front to back if you knew that you could double your vocabulary by doing so?

- Would you sleep with your supervisor for a promotion and a 100 percent increase in salary?

- Would you roll naked in a pig sty for $100?

- Would you spend ten years working in a fast food restaurant if you could then work your dream job for the rest of your life?

- Would you star in a porno movie if the only person you had to have sex with was (name someone famous)?

- Would you sit on a hornets' nest for $5000?

- Would you undergo a free simple operation on your genitalia that would make you multiorgasmic every time you had sex? However, the procedure would be broadcast on a major television network.

- Would you have sex with a member of the same sex in order to have sex with your dream partner?

- Would you snort a line of flour if it gave you the same high as cocaine without posing a threat to your health?

- Would you go to the bathroom in your pants for two days, without changing your clothes, for a $3000 shopping spree at the nearest mall?

- Would you stick a cactus up your butt for a new convertible?

- Would you cut off one of your toes and eat it for a million dollars?

- Would you dive head first, with no scuba gear, into a full outhouse to retrieve a 20-carat diamond?

- Would you work for an Alaskan fishing boat for two years if you could get a full ride scholarship for a masters or doctorate degree in the area of your choice?

- Would you spend half an hour letting a vulture pick at you for $10,000?

- Would you drop a lit firecracker down your pants and let it explode for an opportunity to be on every game show currently on the air?

APPENDIX C.   TRUTHS

- Would you rather drink a pint of your own snot or a teaspoon of another player's snot?

- If you had to sleep with one of the other players, besides a significant other, who would it be?

- If you were to have a homosexual experience with one of your close friends, who would you choose?

- What was your last erotic dream about?

- Would you rather streak through a newsroom during a live telecast or gnaw off an entire fingernail?

- Describe the last time that you pleasured yourself.

- Describe the awkwardness that you experienced during your first sexual experience.

- Describe your most embarrassing sexual experience.

- Give all of the intricate details of your last sexual thought.

- Give all the intricate details of your last trip to the restroom.

- If you had to break another player's arms, who would you choose?

APPENDIX D.   DARES

- Pick another player's nose.

- Make an open-face sandwich using your own face, a slice of bread, and at least three condiments from the refrigerator.

- Moon the other players.

- Kiss another player's bare bottom.

- Drink a raw egg.

- Couch dance for another player.

- Go into the other room and use a ruler to measure your penis and report your findings to the rest of the group. At least one other person must accompany you as a witness to the measurement.

- Call your mother and bark at her over the phone.

- Turn the TV on and impersonate one of the characters on the first show that comes up.

- Pull down your pants and do a head stand.

- Lay on the floor and impersonate an egg frying.

- Drool on yourself.

- Suck on another player's big toe.

- Get in a fight with yourself (you must tell yourself off and throw a couple of punches).

- Pretend to have sex with an inanimate object (pillow, sofa, etc.).

- Lip-sync and dance to a song of your choice.

- Act like you are possessed.

- Sprinkle sugar (or a similar substance) on another players arm, and vacuum it up with your lips.